False Shuffles

P9-BJA-478

FALSE SHUFFLES

Jane Urquhart

Drawings by Tony Urquhart

Press Porcépic
Victoria Toronto

Copyright © 1982 by Jane Urquhart.
All rights reserved.

No part of this book may be reproduced or transmitted in any form by
any means, electronic or mechanical, including photocopying, recording
or any information storage, retrieval and transmission systems now
known or to be invented, without permission in writing from the
publisher, except by a reviewer who may quote brief passages in a
review.

This edition is published by Press Porcépic Ltd., 235–560 Johnson Street,
Victoria, B.C. v8w 3c6, with the assistance of the Canada Council.

Typeset by The Typeworks in Janson.
Printed in Canada by Morriss.

Cover design by Derrick Carter.

1   2   3   4   85   84   83   82

Canadian Cataloguing in Publication Data

Urquhart, Jane, 1949–
    False shuffles

    Poems.
    ISBN 0–88878–204–7

    I. Title..
    PS8591.R69FS   c811'.54   c82–091267–0
    PR9199.3.U77F3

35,847

For Tony and in memory of Paul Keele

CAMROSE LUTHERAN COLLEGE
LIBRARY

Table of Contents

The Undertaker's Bride

Grandmother Crosses   15
The Limit of Suspension   16
The Verandah   17
Departure   19
The Undertaker's Bride   20
War Song   22
Between Brothers   23
The Train to South Dakota   25
Keeping Score   27
Summer Dresses   29

Blood in the Lobby

Martin and the Telescope   37
The Boss   39
Waitresses   40
Fireman   42
Bouncer   44
Compulsory Costume Cupboard   45
Cleaning Ladies' Rag   46
Confused Weather   48
Old Soldier   49
Parking Lot, 2 A.M.   50
Panic   52
Max   54
Mr. Bloombury   56
Four Pitchers of Beer   58
When He Remembers Moonbar   60
Blood Salad   61
Ambulance   63
Final Exit   65

False Shuffles

Top Hat and Tails   73
False Shuffles   74
     i.   74
     ii.   75
     iii.   76
     iv.   77
     v.   79
     vi.   80
     vii.   81
Party Game   83

Tales I'm Not Likely to Tell

Tales I'm Not Likely to Tell   91
   I   (He decides to go to the)   92
   II   (Grandmother's best friend)   93
   III   (At the dinner party)   94
   IV   (They decide to put father in the barn)   95
   V   (I carry Vic's trunk)   96
   VI   (She is walking with him)   98
   VII   (She dies at home)   100
   VIII   (The old man fears dust)   102
   IX   (This lady collects thinkers)   103
   X   (The extended family)   104
   XI   (After spotting a thin perpendicular)   105
   XII   (She goes although she understands)   106
   XIII   (An old lady steals scissors)   107
   XIV   (The night her daughter died)   109
   XV   (He keeps bees)   111
   XVI   (My mother dismantles)   113

The Undertaker's Bride

"The ordinary false shuffle by the dovetail method is scarcely more than an imperfect shuffle which the performer turns to his own advantage."

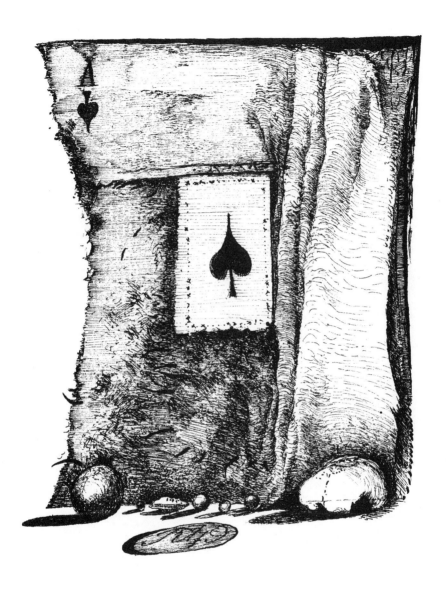

Grandmother Crosses

Grandmother crosses
the suspension bridge

she is seven years old
in the process
of eliminating
            errands

she watches amazed
as the loaf of bread
                she has carried
from the american side
slips from her hands

somersaults gently
to the rapids below

light
        as an angel's gold brick

eighty years later
the streetcars passing
on mainstreet
will bring to her mind
                    this bump of

rubber wheels
on wooden planks

as she rides her tricycle

thinking of home

The Limit of Suspension

On three small scraps of paper
grandmother writes

      how the suspension bridge
      fell down

      how the cotton wool
                crash
      pulled her from
      starched sheets to the
      lung-stopping chill
      of the january night

      how her shoes squeaked
      in the snow

and looking at the
suspension bridge
            lying
broken-backed against the ice
like an injured dragon

                grandmother
must have wondered at
each of her magic crossings

but writes here
        only
the suspension bridge
            fell down

and it did make a noise

The Verandah

Nineteen

hair piled high
afternoons on
the wooden verandah
of Kick's Hotel

     where her mother
     dressed in black
     moves like a cloud
     behind the soft screen door

     fabricating
     tiny wreaths
     from light brown hair

grandmother is passing the time
around like cupcakes at nineteen

rhythms of porch swings
father and brother recently dead
locks of their hair
braided in
mourner's jewellry

summer afternoon

several young men are
tipping their hats to grandmother

sooner or later
grandfather will pass

he is the icing
he is the season

he will die too
of course

men always do

Departure

When grandmother
                    fell in love
for the third time
there were months
of perfectly planned
                    coincidences

                    once his cuff link
                    fell into the river

                    once he whistled
                    adeline

and because she could not
disconnect
time and meaning

events evolved to
cold pure words

written on a photograph
in black and white

                    of grandmother's third love
                    standing near
                                        what's left of
                    table rock

                    looking past
                    the fog of the falls
                    to the american side

                    thinking of departure

Undertaker's Bride

Grandmother
was an undertaker's bride

it couldn't be helped

the profession ran in
her husband's family

she was twenty-one
at the turn of the present century
her name was
                    adeline
just like the song

grandmother kept an intricate
account of
death by water

that was her job

sometimes she described
more than sixty floaters a summer
all of them slipped

over the falls
one way or another

she wrote
their remaining physical
characteristics
            and their
tiny possessions
in a small brown book

it looks as if it couldn't be
helped

        it looks as if
                    somebody
had to write it

War Song

Grandmother has the devil
in her
big as a woodchuck

rationing has been
imposed
so she

rushes to
the dominion store
to buy up all the sugar

before the hoarders
get it

and there will be sweet tea
on afternoons
set aside for the knitting
of regulation dunkirk socks

knit one pearl
two
sweet tea and gasoline
for each of three hearses

business continues as usual

> *good teeth*
> *blue suspenders*
> *regulation dunkirk socks*
> *fingers on left hand*
> *missing*

Between Brothers

A fight starts
in a moment

travels all around the
yard

and ruins roses

involves two or three
dogs who
scare the goldfish

deeper in the pond

a fight speaks of
heat or play
or boredom

a fight lasts an
instant or an afternoon

and always finishes
with the loser in the trough
shaking his head like an animal

(the water scatters
through the vision of
his startled sisters
suddenly blooming
at the kitchen window and

grandmother shouting
as she dries the edges of
her hands

all around her apron)

The Train to South Dakota

The train
        to south dakota
and grandmother sits
on red plush seats
           beside
her eldest son

at home he spends his hours
with his face against
the slippery necks of horses

at home
      and here
he cannot speak

he cannot speak the landscape
passing by the windows
or nights when view
becomes reflection

and other faces in the glass
mingle
with his own

he cannot say
         the moon is in the water of
         the ditch beside the tracks

so all through the journey
grandmother listens
to the abandon of the whistle

and listens day and night
to the wheels
beneath the train

        which say

someone there will fix him
someone there will fix him

Keeping Score

The sunroom
                in the afternoon
escalates beyond light
becoming a perfect timepiece

as she sits there
keeping score
                cultivating
a careful record of that
which the river offered
in the summer of '28

the pen in the inkwell
on the walnut desk
                lifts
in grandmother's fingers
                     emptying

indelible tatoos
permanent labels

hair and teeth and weight

the contents of a pocket
the value of a tie-pin

now
      as dust motes sail
across her vision she pens
the essence
        of a definition
the answer to a question

as beside *number 116*
she writes

body that
      of a small man

Summer Dresses

Later

flowered cups she drinks
her tea from
echo in her summer
dresses

she is an old woman
contemplating
                    unlaced shoes

memory all around her
like the river of that vein
in one thin hand

against a powdered cheek

behind a cedar door
she feels compelled to organize
the souvenir of wardrobe

(her closet
                    dark
with flowered cloth)

she understands the fabrics
of identity
and reaches for the pen again

the document survives for years

Blood in the Lobby

"Instead of the mirror, you can look at the inverted words through a transparent swizzle stick and the result will be the same."

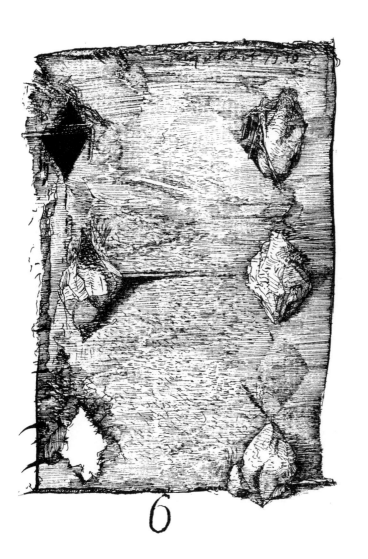

6

Martin and the Telescope

Pay day
       and martin
buys a telescope
on his way
home from the muffler shop

it becomes a thin black beast
resting on his window sill
an extended eye
past the dusty windows of town

but martin soon tires of
pink underwear
even lace
and turns
       in time

to moonbar
following the length of glasses
down along the arborite
until he reaches
rosebud

there are no
properties of air now
between the clutch of
martin's fingers
and the smoke
       which crawls

from rosebud's cigarette
beyond the circle of
his vision

as the lights of town
become a smear on his distorted lens
night becomes a galaxy

(rosebud in the middle
her mind so empty
of his watching)

The Boss

The boss wore a dinner jacket
patterned
with the bulls of altamira

he shouldered his way
through the crowds
like an ambulance

he told us to turn up the music
he told us to turn down the lights
he taught us to stoop
without showing our nipples

he told us
we couldn't wear leather
or choke on
the job

that's all he told us

he was *so* busy
inspecting the stains on the ceiling
he was *so* busy
moving from floor to floor
like an elevator
he was *so* familiar
with skies of neon
acres of vinyl landscape

that he closed his eyes once
and swallowed
the environment

Waitresses

Some of them carried their trays
like valuable art objects
covered all over with
celadon glazes

some of them carried their trays
like offerings
destined for the altar
of throat and stomach

(one of them carried her tray
like an expected accident)

some of them carried their hearts
on their trays
for all the boys in the band

but me
I carried my tray
like tin
and glass

even when I couldn't
price
the objects on it

even when I couldn't
name them

I carried my tray
like the tin
and glass
it really was

under the stars
up to the stage
to all the performers
at moonbar

Fireman

Start with the hat

give him a hat
the one he always wanted
pin on a badge
brighter than christmas

then give him a coat
lined with asbestos
and waterproof
make sure that it covers
each part of his body
make sure it is black
has buckles

give him a ladder
give him a truck
give him a dalmation dog
called sparky

make sure it has teeth

then give him something
hot
to push his
shoulders into

he is not interested
in kittens trapped in trees
he is not interested in grass fires
he is not interested
in administering oxygen
to cardiac patients

give him molten lava
melting boxcars
rivers of scarlet metal

let his lungs singe
let his eyebrows disappear
let his brain begin to bubble
give him something

heated to remember
this man
this fire man

his disappointed eyes are often
filled with tears

Bouncer

You
are the bouncer
at the back
glowing under scarlet
exit signs

your arms are folded
across the wrought
iron of your ribs

your eyes are moving
like a searchlight
into the secrets
the heart of the room

you know the way
that hair adheres to scalp
how the bone tears flesh
as fast as falcons

you claim that
you can smell a knife
can see it shine
in the hustler's shoe

you know as surely
as wages in your wallet

they can start a fight at moonbar
they can't win a fight at moonbar

Compulsory Costume Cupboard

We would have been happy
to wear
the iron railings
from the stairs

we would have been happy
with plaster casts

but beside the punch clock
to the left of the switchboard
was the compulsory
costume cupboard

the boss called this part
of the lobby
pick and punch

black net nightmare
frozen in time

he never did have much
of a sense of humour

The Cleaning Ladies' Rag

Pull up a chair and let's talk
about the cleaning ladies' rag
it's easy when you know the steps
it will miraculously cure your shyness
it will give you confidence
in parts of your body that you
didn't know existed it will in short
change your life

you will travel the line
of the dance around the room
you will learn both the forward
and the backward basic
you will become familiar with the floor
you will be wise about waxing
and stain control

you will swivel from the hip
you will bend at the knee
you will ripple and flicker
and gain new recognition
in your social set

mornings at moonbar
cleaning ladies glide behind
the glass like figure skaters
they prance through
last night's sediment
they've memorized the flush
the scrape the rinse the swab
finally
the intricate rag

it sets them above and apart
their clothes do not constrict
their grace is unsurpassed

their dance halls
when they come to them

shine

Confused Weather

There were nights like that

we'd pull aside the heavy
curtain by the window
watch the snowploughs
rearrange
the parking lot

watch the snow
turn blue inside
the street light

you never made any money
on the outside aisles
on nights like that

confused weather

business kind of slow
tables flat and empty

ice rinks in the dark

so mostly we'd just hang
around the bar on nights
like that
sneaking double shots

kind of bored
kind of restless

talking blood

Old Soldier

By now

he could have been a general
sitting in a garden
somewhere east of edinburgh

retired

throwing pebbles in
a fish pond
thinking of the gunfire and
the girls
sipping golden scotch

not drinking canadian
rye whiskey
night times
in a tattered night club
selling air conditioners
day times

spitting out the sales pitch
like broken teeth

somewhere
slightly east of edinburgh
fish caught in the
                        prison of
their pond
twitching from sharp pebbles

that might as well be bullets

Parking Lot, 2 A.M.

This is the arena
and the audience

this is where
silent cruisers
full of silver-eyed police
never arrive

in time
this is where
lincoln continental trunks
open to reveal
unpleasant passengers

still puddles reflect
broken neon words
buses sail by
full of sad old men
destined for furnished rooms

there are those who leave here
wrapped up in a golden
jacket of guilt

there are those who never leave
who travel asphalt parking lots
for centuries

two hundred keys
glitter nervously
in search of locks

this is where
                    time
and again
a limited knowledge of the weapon
is enhanced
by a genuine knowledge of the hunter

Panic

Any more than
five hundred and forty-seven people
at moonbar
was dangerous

and unlawful

this was because of panic

panic had no purpose
no permanent place of employment
so panic
          was a possibility
everywhere

we were told to assume
a quiet commanding
demeanor
when panic joined the crowd
we were told
to locate by eye
various private and foolproof
means of escape

but panic proved
to be
a maudlin drunk
                    lonely and blubbering
searching all around the stage
up and down the stairs
in the bathrooms
for a workable catastrophe

we walked confidently
towards the exits

were met with walls of fire

no hoses in our hands

Max

He returns to these rooms
after four long years

with the fact of the accident
slung across his shoulders

like serious luggage

he orders whiskey milkshakes
he orders whiskey sandwiches
he organizes fabric on
the bright sea of his belly

max laughing
max singing
max speaking

          everything he might have
          why he doesn't now

knowing there is broken glass
embedded in his shoes
that the accident is permanent

we move to him
wait there
empty all his ashes

until max takes his accident
back into the night

         and we stack trays
         mop down
         sweep up

listen for

the grind
       and then the purr
of his motor in the lot

Mr. Bloombury

i

Because he was both toymaker
and embalmer
each of his nights he described
in miniature the bodies which
over the years the river had
given up for his inspection

his mending

gradually his mind became
a series of appendectomy scars
clothing labels
and whatever the dentist had to say

dangerously mixed with model train parts
and glass eyes for dolls

ii

nights spent at moonbar
he liked miss nude canada the very best
imagined her clockwise on the slab
bloated by river and identifiable
by silicone

watched her through seven
shots and splits
knew that she sang out of tune
arranged his life accordingly
went home to the
human debris that washed
over the cataracts

went home to the tiny world of
the children's train with
its tunnels and roadsigns

thinking of miss nude canada
identifiable as flesh
so entirely lacking in scars

Four Pitchers of Beer

I was about to move from
sleight of hand
to mental mysteries

you were leaving vegetables
and heading into meats

I was making a map of the
parking lot
you were editing a subdivision

I was drying off a draught glass

you were mopping up
the blood
that hid the lobby floor

I was dreaming of
tropical vacations

you were putting your last dime
into the juke box

you showed me what the customers wore
on the dark side of their shoes

you were the last tip
the silver coin
lodged in the windpipe

I would have walked
around the world for you
around the world for you

with four pitchers of beer
on my tray

CAMROSE LUTHERAN COLLEGE
LIBRARY

When He Remembers Moonbar

The hockey game was lost
or won
rock bands appeared and yelled
and thumped and went
away again
the girls walked up and down

the aisles in squeaky shoes
coins shifting on
the edges of their trays

nothing ever happened

no awesome journeys
no desperate phonecalls

just prolonged jukebox
and beads of moisture
sliding from his glass to
table top

she never met him at moonbar

there is nothing to remember

Blood Salad

It's not the first time I've seen blood
in the lobby
      Rosebud, Coronet Lounge, April '77

Rosebud knows the recipe
for blood salad

someone she was fond of
taught her years ago

she never forgot

you wouldn't either

tonight there is
awareness of the documented
ingredients

tonight there is a smell of
draught beer
on her hands
her hair
the click of her heels
on bathroom tile

rosebud is
        descending
a two a.m. staircase

tonight her costume is
detailed
and absurd

tonight there is someone
down there in the lobby
mixing

blood salad

Ambulance

White dove on wheels
with bottles strung like wind chimes
underneath your ribs
up and down your belly

white dove
with the scream of a hawk

inside you
there is theater
there are glass-cased liquids
shifting flat
crazier than the tilt
of fun house floors

the quick-fingered attendant
moving muscle
setting bone

friendly rubber snakes
sucking on an arm

ambulance
your delicate red lightning
traveling my midnight wall
is all that comfort
ever meant to be

                    this knowledge
that even here
even now
there is someone out there
somewhere
left to call

Final Exit

Leaving them
I tried to be dramatic
bought drinks all round
and sent out for pizza

thought of speeches
and rejected them
offered cigarettes
like talismans

before I turned
towards the exit
we all knew I was gone

they were adding up
the evening's take
I was thinking of the door

a failed barmaid
moving into
fresher false careers

leaving them
the muscle of their music
fell over me
like ice cubes from the bar

where they were living it
            just living it

documenting nothing

False Shuffles

"This is a real false shuffle. It will require considerable practice to render it deceptive."

Top Hat and Tails

It's clear to her
that the chauffeur magician undertaker
doorman violinist groom
and the one who comes
to take her to the ball

all dress the same
so how is she to know
whose foot is by the door

one drives her off to tricky destinations
one opens up the door
one plays the mystic music
one escorts her to the floor
one waits for her beside the altar
one fools her with a king or knave
one kisses her behind the curtain
one ushers in the mourners
and digs her shallow grave

singing digging bowing driving
fooling tapping all around the stage
coat tails flying top hat shining
tempo rising feet ablaze

she's come to understand the costume
its unlikely that she'll ever keep the pace

False Shuffles
for Sam Patch†

i

To be a silver needle
quickening
our weakened pulse

to be the single plaster saint
speaking through the lint
inside our pockets

to be the method of transportation
and the destination
the tour guide on all of our
astonishing vacations

the scenic postcard
carefully mailed home

to be the tune we hummed compulsively

a candle lit in fear
beneath obscure cathedrals

he stops for coffee
at an all-night diner
prints his own initials
in the steam that lines the window
pulls a schedule of reason
from the fabric of his
jacket

† Sam Patch was a Niagara daredevil who successfully jumped the falls
several times until he tried it drunk in the dark on a dare. This time he
killed himself. *J. U.*

then his shoes are ships
upon the floor
then his purpose is the path
outside our door

ii

She believed that the deck
was unmarked
she believed that the hat
was empty
she believed that the doves
and the rabbits were real

magical and holy

she knew he could follow
the history of objects by smell

she trusted his abrupt
                    night fires

iii

she remembers footlights
causing a bright white curtain
to close across the audience
she remembers stage dust
clinging to the static of
her patent leather shoes
chalk marks mapping out
the distance

smiles steps
gestures revolutions

she remembers perspiration
stains ruining the satin
he chose for her

and that's not all he
chose for her

necklaces of fear
corsets of desire

she remembers
the band of black
he wound around his hat

the audience hollering
for molsen's golden

all around the hall

iv

while voltage carried current
over broken arms of
stainless steel
                        lighting up
the tools
            his teeth
the table
she carried his illusions

      handkerchiefs and playing cards
      silver coins and swizzle sticks

ordinary objects
without him

how she wished
she were a waitress
delivering dental tools
to the crowd

           how she wished
she were a nurse
serving knives

              opening nights
             matinees
the pressure of her flesh
behind the gridwork of her costume

his smile that hovered
just above her shoulder

soon he would force
her to vanish
empty the contents of her tray

illusions

and black net of her stocking
still glued against her side

v

He leaps from anything
to anywhere
for the amusement of the ladies

he jumps from the edge of
entertainment
                scribbling his victories
on the sky's black board
confident his daylight instinct
can renegotiate
his secret pact with
gravity

and yet tonight

there are these stains
on his biography

this unremarkable costume

as he's caught
              turning
in the wind towards
the earth's magnet

caught turning
to what now becomes the fall

this long unbroken
contract
cast in granite
by the dark

79

vi

He was always other
something untouched   fractional
rising from the dark
along the ditches
and leaving her

later in the journey
wondering
wondering
was it really him

shining through the dark
like irregular diamonds
causing the needle of the gauge
to rise higher   faster
like the needle inside her brain
that played him
and played him

leaving her
wondering
was it really him
or merely a bracelet of snow
slung over a highway
harder than bullets

was it really him

or merely his grave
and something beyond it

vii

Among the wonders of the flesh
the marvels of biology
there was morning

always morning
the real landscape
coming into focus
just behind
the scenery of dreams

pushing the crockery across
the table
into regular configurations
settings for
first one man
then another

        her hands
work out from
lace trim at her wrists

first one man
then another

and morning
moving to the weapon
of pure cutlery

sunny side up

"Practise the sleight until you can do it naturally and easily. You will be surprised how simple it is—and how deceptive."

Party Game

He arrives in time
with a silver tray

on it he has placed
the skull of a squirrel
a postcard of niagara
a saint christopher medal
a broken draught glass
part of a velvet curtain
an insurance policy
last week's bank statement
an escargot fork
a boy scout badge
his baby teeth
a lottery ticket
a rejection slip
a champagne cork
a deck of cards

remember these objects
he tells her
with tears in his voice

remember these objects

AND WRITE THEM ALL DOWN

Tales I'm not Likely to Tell

"It reaches a point where just the slightest twist enables the magician to change a genuine shuffle into a false one."

Tales I'm not Likely to Tell

At night they clutter up my dreams
gazing out to me
like renaissance portraits
while landscape shifts
behind them into shadow

these beings are the people
in the dreams my mother told me
or figures of dark episodes
connected by my grandmother

light is thrown over them
they grow attain
the breadth of secrets
of stories not told
of stories when told
not told correctly

I'm left with fragments
this one's hair
                that one's death
memory's natural selection
building on detail
disposing of the rest

                    until they come
to be just this
characters I'm unable to give shape to
tales I'm not likely to tell
loose bits of paper carried by the wind

caught for a moment
on the fence around this time

I

He decides to go to the
neighbouring village

about a hundred years ago

it is a long journey
involving

time and dust
passing through the swamp
he is robbed by highwaymen
they take his uninitialed
pocket watch

and seven shining quarters

that evening
as the sun collapses
into the horizon
he decides to leave off
making cabinets
become an undertaker
making boxes

he is an ancestor of mine

to this day
I know my burglars
better than my carpenters

II

Grandmother's best friend
drowns herself at nineteen
pregnant
in a shallow stream

for years the town wonders
if this is possible

face down and covered by
an old dark dress
she does not resemble
ophelia
         does not even
consider
the lady of shallot

inhales more
mud than water
minnows too
                and swamp grasses
growing to the sun

grandmother thinks of this
while she is not swimming

for all the years after

III

At the dinner party
I am seated between
the cure for cancer

and domestic bliss

the room is immense
so is the fireplace
the food continues
no one flicks pearls

from one end of the table
to the other
and this is just as well

when I begin to sing
show tunes
domestic bliss
becomes a chorus

the cure for cancer
falls down drunk
upon the floor
my husband takes me home

early

IV

They decide to put father in the barn
for the summer
make him sleep on straw

he does not object
likes the look of grain dust
traveling the sun track
from wood seam
to the floor

several distant relatives
discuss this in a kitchen far away
they cannot understand

why an old man should share
his final months with dairy cows
but late at night

a single star shines through
the space between two boards
and bounces back a beam
from his left eye

V

I carry Vic's trunk
around with me always everywhere
in my mind

he is dead
his trunk is missing
we have never met

something happened long ago
perhaps a horse kicked him
in the head

I have cleaned out
the entire house
given the icons to the salvation army
cut the grass
carted it away

I have eaten all the chives
in the garden

sometimes I carry the trunk's
environment as well
the linoleum it rested on
the window that it stood beneath
three hundred droning cluster flies
littering the sill

          I vacuum these
the machine hums
for days

a blue fir tree moves
back and forth in the wind

I remember Vic
no one else does

VI

She is walking with him
through streets
in france

      they enter
a wide boulevard
which intersects architecture

he stops to photograph a wall
she looks down

to the end of the avenue
where the merry-go-round
dressed in neon
goes on and on
           at the end
of the street
which is the end of the town
and there are hills

beyond this
      his shadow
is long in the sun
but a filthy cloud
as solid as clay
announces itself at the back
of the emerald landscape

she knows
exactly what will happen
we do too

that night
while they are eating their oysters
the lights go out

all over the restaurant

VII

She dies at home
then leaves the room
to fly over the village
with her husband
and full-grown son

from this distance
the cracks she avoided
on sidewalks
appear as gentle
as ruled pencil lines

the children file out
from the school door
she notices their parts are straight
their hair shines

the church is locked
shingles are missing
from its pointed roof
the eaves troughs are full
of damp brown leaves
which have fallen from

the extended arms
of dark dark trees
the men murmur
one to each ear
their arms are as weightless

as threads on a loom
suddenly she remembers
a pink lace handkerchief
given her as a child

she wants to return for it

for three days
the villagers speak
of winds from the south
spiced with cologne

VIII

The old man fears dust
knows civilizations
have been buried by it
can cite examples

the old woman sends birthday cards
to movie stars
likes the colours of balloons
and small wax candles
thinks he's crazy

they live in a clapboard house
filled with valuable objects
he hoards these
she licks stamps
they own cats

the old man buys rulers
to measure dust accumulation
he believes that archeologists
are romantic young men
with black capes and shovels

they both keep brooms
close by them always

like prayers

IX

This lady collects thinkers
they sit in her parlour
on straight-backed chairs

they talk about really living
how her sons would rather watch
hockey

finally she falls in love
with one
they sleep beneath the stars
in a down-filled sack

he goes insane

later she collects fish

X

The extended family
extends
beyond her hopes and fears

they buy up cottages
all round the lake
often hold regattas

they cut a chapel
into the rocks
sing hymns

finally they all intermarry
produce a brand new product
for the evolutionary showcase

she never catches the bouquet

she moves out west

raises elkhounds
instead

XI

After spotting a thin perpendicular
line of smoke above the trees
I discover the skunk charmer's
cabin in the woods

I open the door
who are you ?
                we ask
each other simultaneously

I am immersed in an amazing city
the architecture resembles
nothing I've ever seen
we discuss

the ownership of land
                        the refrigerator
the usefulness of old
toothless men

defeated I go home

two weeks later the skunks arrive
and the next day the skunk charmer
well? he says

fortunately I enjoy the smell
of skunks dead

on dusty roads
at midnight

XII

She goes although she understands
she will not be asked
to dance

she huddles in a corner
with some other girls
her face filled with shame
and braces

she leaves before the lights
come up
and walks the long sidewalk
to her home

            entering
the house alone
she watches all the furniture
take shape inside the dark
and hears the
sudden roar
of the basement furnace

activated
by the cold
that entered with her
through the door

XIII

An old lady steal scissors
it is a full time occupation

she drags them home
at the end of each day
in a shopping cart she has
also stolen
precisely for this purpose

this was not as easy
grocers are suspicious

her room is an eternity of scissors
unending scissors
her walls glisten
with ovals and blades

once when she thought she'd have
chicken pie for dinner
she opened the door of the oven
and an avalanche of scissors
descended to the floor

which was already covered
with scissors

she ate out

oddly enough
she never cuts anything

but we know
                    nothing
of her past

XIV

The night her daughter died
she bridled horses
and drove the old sleigh
two miles
to her son-in-law's farm

where she loaded the hope
chest onto the horsehair
and left
without dialogue

the baby died too

her return was complex
a tremendous blizzard
swept over the acres
owned by her husband
landscape faded to white
then reappeared
like an unexpected wall

she let go of the reins
blind horses
                    moved home
into the stables

I am not born for a long
long time
            but
will later discover
an elderly chest filled with
pillow slips quilt squares
and doilies

and my mother will speak
about weather

XV

He keeps bees
and lives with his aunt
who eventually dies

great round bushes
hug the foundations
of his house and blossom
into winter dark

spring comes
he rakes and trims
and the tiny legs of bees awaken
fragile
from their programmed
winter sleep

he cuts firewood and tills
a market garden
he dismantles
split rail fences

which he'll use for kindling
when something of the autumn
moves around the cornerstone
then at night

he will walk outside
beneath the vast cup
of sky and wait

until he singles out
the particular smell
of delicate bees
about to drowse

XVI

My mother dismantles
a cast lead tombstone
when she is nine years old

her brother has told her
the old lady's clothes
are bundled in there

it is empty of course
she loses three bolts
is unable to reassemble

it properly
it tilts to the left
and panels of lead
groan in the wind

for decades to come
it is one of the marks
she has left
on the landscape

the document survives for years

Some of these poems have been published in *Fiddlehead*, *The Antigonish Review*, *Prism International*, *The Malahat Review* and *Four Square Garden, an Anthology.*

All quotes are from *Blackstone's Tricks Anyone Can Do*, Garden City Publishing Co., New York, 1948